Dartmouth

David Bradley and Shelby Grantham, editors

Published by Dartmouth College

Distributed by University Press of New England

Hanover and London

Dartmouth

The University Press of New England
is a consortium of universities in New England dedicated to
publishing scholarly and trade works by authors from member
campuses and elsewhere. The New England imprint signifies
uniform standards for publication excellence maintained
without exception by the consortium members. A joint
imprint of University Press of New England and a sponsoring
member acknowledges the publishing mission of that
university and its support for the dissemination of scholarship
throughout the world. Cited by the American Council of
Learned Societies as a model to be followed, University Press
of New England publishes books under its own imprint and
the imprints of
Brandeis University
Brown University
Clark University
University of Connecticut
Dartmouth College
University of New Hampshire
University of Rhode Island
Tufts University
University of Vermont
Wesleyan University

Designed by Sally Harris and produced by
Summer Hill Books, Perkinsville, Vermont.

Printed in the United States of America   ∞

Library of Congress Cataloging-in-Publication Data

Dartmouth / David Bradley and Shelby Grantham, editors.
    p. cm.
  ISBN 0-87451-494-0
    1. Dartmouth College — Description — Views.   2. Dartmouth College —
History.   I. Bradley, David, 1915-   .   II. Grantham, Shelby.
LD1439.7.D37   1990
378.742'3 — dc20   89-28479
                                                                          CIP

5 4 3 2 1

Dedicated
to archivists
Anne Scotford and Kenneth Cramer

Sine quibus non.

You know that life has never made complete sense to any thoughtful person and, yet, that it makes too much sense to be left either to chance or to fools. Hence education.

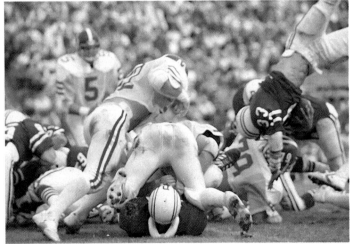

Matriculation

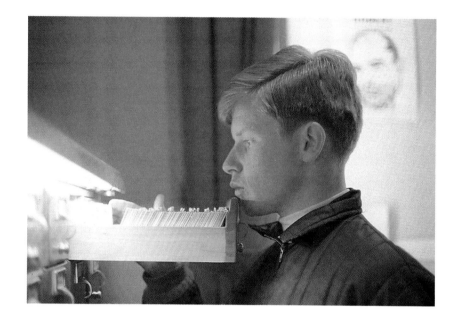

Leaf Kicking

Of course there is music. There was always music and words and singing, memories and visions like a wind-harvest on a bright October day.

Hence these pictures — a small gathering from more than two hundred autumns, from Eleazar's empty wilderness to the bewildering worldliness of the modern Dartmouth. Thirty-four artists and photographers, most of them professional, some amateurs, have left us this whirldown. They invite us to go leaf kicking. I propose to accept, see what we turn up.

First thing I notice in these pictures are the happy, young faces. Everything good under the sun is here: the libraries, the laboratories, the teachers, the leisure time for exploring and learning in the long white afternoons or solitary midnights.

This is a prosperous Dartmouth, now in its third century — a large college, with a multitude of those who love it. Nothing of the log-cabin school carved from a wilderness two hundred years ago remains. Nothing of the raw provincial college of a hundred years ago remains, when cows and pigs had to be chased from the green so that baseball could be played.

Nothing but the shape of the hills, the north-south sliding gleam of the river, and the spirit of the place.

The spirit hasn't changed much in two centuries. The prototype Dartmouth student wrote his shout from the hills in the third year of the college. His words could have served as the Freshman Handbook in 1772; they would do pretty well today:

I took my axe with me, and such articles of clothing and a few such books as were necessary. . . .

Something happens to young men and women up here. It can't be preached or planned or taught; it just happens:

Maybe on a freshman trip where, scrambling over the slabs of a shattered ridge on Washington or Passaconaway, they find themselves looking across 12,000 years into the face of the ice age;

Or, crowding into a classroom for the first time, they hear all the impossible things expected of them: the books, the experiments, computers, research, the papers — the thinking they'll have to do. (Milton, for example. Has anyone yet figured out what to think about Milton?);

Or discovering the books of Baker Library, the arts of the Hood Museum and Hopkins Center;

Or alone some midnight, standing in the great white cold among five billion years of stars.

Something happens. When we next hear of these people, they've been exploring the Ross ice shelf or running the surf on the Sandwich Islands, paddling the Dubawnt or forcing a route on the west ridge of Everest, inventing a kidney machine or writing a book of poems.

But of all unexpected things, the oddest is this: that there was ever a Dartmouth College in this place.

Take a tiny Indian school in Connecticut, declare it to be a college, uproot it, lug it (along with a handful of Delawares and Mohawks) two hundred miles north in carts and wagons, beyond all reach of civilization, beyond the Deerfield settlements and Fort No. 4, to a wilderness riverbank in the Hampshire Grants. Try to raise money in England. Take your chances on the time: 1770. (It is seven years after the last Indian uprising; five years before the Revolution.) Begin the felling and clearing in late July.

God's blessing was on Eleazar Wheelock and his small crew of tutors and students, for the cold weather held off almost through December. When snow came, they had two log cabins fairly well closed in. Instruction could begin: prayers at dawn, morning recitations in Latin, Greek, mathematics, and the Bible, further recitations in the afternoon, prayers at dark.

The following August, Eleazar was ready with his first commencement. He invited Governor Wentworth to ride over from Wolfeboro for the ceremonies. The class composed a graduation anthem — the first Dartmouth song.

When he proclaimed the curses of the law . . . the
pulpit was clothed in thunder, the coruscations of
truth were as forked lighting. . . . When he
addressed the humble saint, his voice was that of
angels who welcome the spirits of the just to
mansions not made with hands.

O Eleazar Wheelock perpius erat vir.

Yesterday morning I got up at 6:45 and did my housework till 7:00, and then studied geometry till 7:30. Ate breakfast and went to chapel till 8:10 and then recited geometry till 9. Studied Greek till 11, and recited till 12. Then prayer meeting till 12:30 and dinner till 1. Played till 2 and studied Latin till 2:30. Gymnastics till 3, and studied Latin till 5 and recited till 6. Supper till 6:30 and geometry till 8:30. Then a classmate came and visited me a little while and I wrote a letter and went to bed at 10.

The classical curriculum continued almost unchanged for 120 years, rigorous, restrictive, and ever more obsolete—until President Tucker designed the bridge to the modern curriculum.

෨෨෨Undaunted spirit. We needed it again a hundred years later. The final demise of farming in the north country carried the rural college along with it. By 1890, Dartmouth was little better off than Eleazar's Indian school had been. It had little money, few prospects, and 315 students.

No matter: it had devoted alumni and, over the next nine decades, four remarkable presidents. Together they fashioned the modern college celebrated in these pictures.

One started as a teacher of sacred rhetoric. He became a master designer of modern education and wizard of finance. One was a businessman so sure of his conservatism that he was not afraid of being liberal. The third was a State Department expert: he knew the great issues of our time, knew they must be brought into the classrooms. The fourth was a mathematician, a refugee from totalitarian Europe: he believed in justice and obligation in Eleazar's old-fashioned way.

They transformed the college into the national and international institution it now is. They turned it into a college for daughters, sisters, and mothers as well. They were great leaders because Opportunity dared them to be bigger than themselves and they accepted the dare.

Yet all their vision and courage would have come to nothing had it not been for the hundreds of trustees and thousands of alumni and alumnae who did the work. They skidded out the logs, poured the foundations. They may not have turned on the lights, but they laid the power lines.

Behind the designers and the builders, barely noticed in the long, cool shadows, are Dartmouth's dreamers: the poets, the musicians. They formed our impulses into words. They gave singing to our spirits. Miraculously.

D.B.

Hanover Winter Song

Ho, a song by the fire! Pass the pipes, pass the bowl;
Ho, a song by the fire! With a skoal, with a skoal!
Ho, a song by the fire! Pass the pipes, with a skoal!
For the wolf-wind is wailing at the doorways,
And the snow drifts deep along the road,
And the ice-gnomes are marching from their Norways,
And the great white cold walks abroad.

For here by the fire
    We defy frost and storm.
Ha, Ha! We are warm,
    And we have our heart's desire.
For here's four good fellows,
    And the beechwood and the bellows,
And the cup is at the lip
    In the pledge of fellowship.

Pile the logs on the fire! Fill the pipes, pass the bowl;
Pile the logs on the fire! With a skoal, with a skoal!
Pile the logs on the fire! Fill the pipes, with a skoal!
For the fire-goblins flicker on the ceiling,
And the wine-witch glitters in the glass,
And the smoke-wraiths are drifting, curling, reeling,
And the sleigh-bells jingle as they pass.

Lyrics by Richard Hovey, Class of 1885
Music by Frederic F. Bullard

The Alma Mater

Dear old Dartmouth! Give a rouse
For the college on the hill!
For the Lone Pine above her,
And the loyal ones who love her,
Give a rouse, give a rouse, with a will!
For the sons of old Dartmouth,
For the daughters of Dartmouth,
Though 'round the girdled earth they roam,
Her spell on them remains;
They have the still North in their hearts,
The hill-winds in their veins,
And the granite of New Hampshire
In their muscles and their brains.

Dear old Dartmouth! Set a watch
Lest the old traditions fail!
Stand as sister stands by brother!
Dare a deed for the old Mother!
Greet the world, from the hills, with a hail!
For the sons of old Dartmouth,
For the daughters of Dartmouth,
Around the world they keep for her
Their old undying faith;
They have the still North in their soul,
The hill-winds in their breath;
And the granite of New Hampshire
Is made part of them till death.

Lyrics by Richard Hovey, Class of 1885
Music by Harry R. Wellman '07

DARTMOUTH COLLEGE
HANOVER NEW HAMPSHIRE

Dartmouth Undying

Dartmouth! – There is no music for our singing,
no words to bear the burden of our praise,
yet how can we be silent and remember
The splendor and the fullness of her days!

Who can forget her soft September sunsets,
Who can forget those hours that passed like dreams –
The long cold shadows floating on the campus,
The drifting beauty where the twilight streams?

Who can forget her sharp and misty mornings,
The clanging bells, the crunch of feet on snow,
Her sparkling noons, the crowding into Commons,
Her long white afternoons, her twilight glow?

See! By the light of many thousand sunsets
Dartmouth Undying like a vision starts:
Dartmouth – the gleaming, dreaming walls of Dartmouth
miraculously builded in our hearts.

Franklin McDuffee

21

PAUL SAMPLE

Dr. Tucker's College
(1893–1909)

1883 campus. This (with the addition of Rollins Chapel, Butterfield dorm, and Webster Hall) is what President Tucker saw when he walked his campus. But what he and Mr. Hopkins envisioned across this wide green sward was a library. A library beyond all imaginings, beyond any glimmer of financing. It took twenty years to plan, and nine buildings had to be moved or demolished.

1791
1904
1934

*In these latter days there has developed a theory
called evolution. I have thoroughly and critically
examined this theory and find it is absolutely false.*

President Samuel Colcord Bartlett

*When we realize that evolution is the summation of
power through cooperation, that what we call "evil"
is that which prevents or destroys cooperation, and
good is that which perpetuates or improves
cooperation; when we realize that the "struggle for
existence" is a struggle to find better ways and
means of cooperation, and that the "fittest" is the
one that cooperates best — we shall then realize that
science and religion and government stand on
common ground and have a common purpose.*

Professor of Biology William Patten

Mr. Hopkins' College
(1916–1945)

And see now,
here is that place, those greens
are here, deep with those blues. The air
we breathe is freshly sweet, and warm, as though
with berries. We are here. We are here.
Set this down, too, as much
as if an atrocity had happened and been seen.
The earth is beautiful beyond all change.

I have come to distrust the validity of much of what has been said, including much which I have said myself.

Get the right word! Get it the first time!

*In 1924, the cagey philanthropist
George F. Baker asked:
"What can you do with $25,000?"
"Not much," replied Mr. Hopkins,
gambling.*

$2,132,000

*In 1930, his last year, Mr. Baker looked out on the
campus from the colonnade of the Library.
"Dartmouth is a good college," he mused.
"Everybody speaks well of Dartmouth."*

Poet

It was hard even to think of Christmas in that atmosphere of barbed wire and bayonets, they said. They were sick and starved and lonely and forgotten. There were no Christmas letters, no packages, no tree, no hope even. They tried to put Christmas out of their minds. But very early on that Christmas morning, before it was light, the camp wakened to the unaccustomed sound of singing. A handful of men gathered in the dark outside the barracks, and as their fellow prisoners listened they sang, very softly, the Dartmouth Winter Song. The homesick Americans lay on the bare filthy boards and listened to that universal song of the north wind and snow and the great white cold, the beechwood and the bellows and the pledge of fellowship, and it brought some things close that had been very far away. They listened in silence, and the only sound in the dark was when a man began to cry.

Orozco would come up periodically and talk over his plans with me, and so forth.

And when he got to that panel on the sterility of education, he says, "Look," he says, "I've been treated too well here to do this. I want to talk it over with you."

"Nothing doing," I says. "You've taken everybody else in the world over the hurdles, and we aren't going to ask any immunity at all on the thing."

President Hopkins

I want to see the College filled with visible symbols of spiritual and intellectual things. . . . I want a carillon to play just as the sun falls below the Vermont hills and dusk comes on.

Mr. Dickey's College
(1945–1970)

A lot of Dartmouth people are owned by dogs.
President John Sloan Dickey belongs to a big golden
retriever, who sits beside the President's desk in the
Administration Building all day and walks him
home every night on a leash, to make sure that Dr.
Dickey doesn't run away.

Don't hit him until I drop the puck.

Coach

"This," said Ike, "is what a college ought to look like."

No one is asking to see poetry regularized in courses and directed by coaches like sociology and football. . . . But it does seem as if it could be a little more connived at than it is. I, for one, should be in favor of the college's setting the expectation of poetry forward a few years (the way clocks are set forward in May) so as to get young poets started earlier in the morning before the freshness dries off.

Deans

The wartime issue, however complex in its origin, was starkly simple; it was "we or they" and to the finish. The issues of peacetime are different. They are numerous, complex, and ill-defined, . . . the business of the truly educated man, and it is a harder business than you imagine.

The Modern College
(1970–   )

Love is twice warm in a cold place.

Softly now the early twilight
Thro' the trees is stealing down,
And the evening hush is falling
O'er the college and the town.

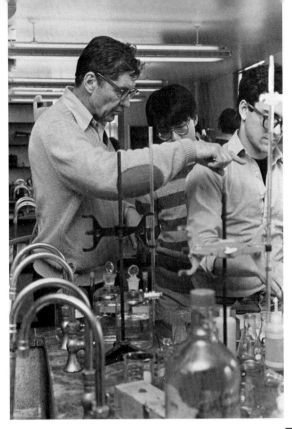

The terrible eyes

. . . the soft voices.

*The only trouble with facts is that there are
too many of them.*

Arctic barrens,
professor paddling bow,
student in the stern,
teachers everywhere.

A college, like a coral harbor, builds up year by year, generation by generation, crisis by crisis, benefaction by benefaction, dedicated man by dedicated man until, out of its own accumulation of experienced truth, a sanctuary arises where the meaning and beauty of other times and climes may say their say to ours and be heard.

And yet, good friend and esteemed successor, be not dismayed — as a wise man once said: "Nothing succeeds like successors."

A liberal education encourages students to discover and affirm their most authentic selves. It enables them to reflect independently on the nature and texture of their lives. It inspires them to delineate a moral identity and to seek balance and proportion. With our help, they develop the empathy and courage required to endure uncertainty, anxiety, and suffering. In the end, we challenge them to go forth, glad in their knowledge and convictions, to make a difference in this world.

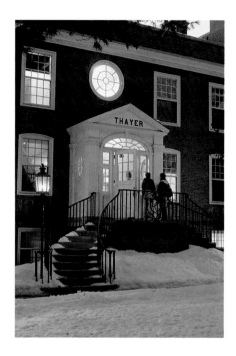

The essence of Thayer.

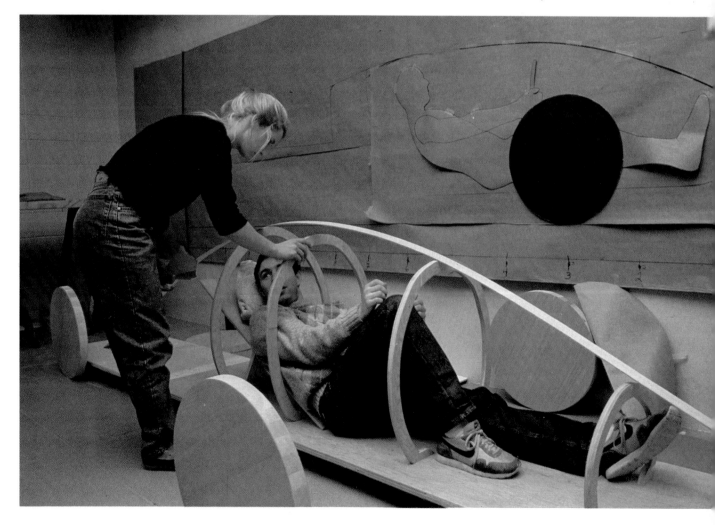

The Quinntessence of Tuck.

So accustomed was I to the noise of Cambridge traffic, that the odd sound of snowflakes smashing onto the earth kept me awake all night.

Tuesday Morning

"The student has nerves," explained a Dartmouth professor in 1926, "and he sometimes bays at the moon. He is subject to lunar rages which arise from dead calm, swell almost to mob violence and subside without a trace."

At first, student rages were about the food. In 1774 they got so bad that Governor Wentworth himself had to intervene. Then it was cows. Townspeople were grazing cattle on the Green, and the undergraduates kidnapped and held the animals hostage in the cellar of Dartmouth Hall, standing off town, gown, and president until promised a playing field without pies. Eighteen hundred and twenty-four was a particularly nervy year, during which the scholars burned a barn, stoned a professor, and strung up the president in effigy.

But the most extravagant protest in the annals of Dartmouth was the work of its trustees. They caused a ruckus that spread to the faculty, swept up students, and set the stage for the most famous dissenter in American college history—a 36-year-old Dartmouth alumnus.

The year was 1815, the issue ownership. President John Wheelock felt that the college was his by primogeniture, and he had appealed to the state for support against a board of trustees who thought otherwise. The canny New Hampshire legislators backed Wheelock on the grounds that when the colony became a state, the colonial college became a university—and theirs to bestow. Inflamed trustees and faculty promptly denounced the president, liberated the library in a night raid, and declared an alternative campus.

Their sit-in lasted three years and wasted the college to bare bone and defiance. But the United States Supreme Court heard Daniel Webster's impassioned argument and decided for the trustees. "It is, Sir," declared Webster, "a small college. And yet, there are those who love it!"

Alumni have also proved restless under full moons. Middle-aged graduates cried "Degenerate!" and cut the college out of wills when bathtubs were installed in dormitories. Alumni agitated so fiercely for a voice in college affairs that in 1891 they won the right to elect five out of twelve trustees. It was their growling over Orozco's gory paintings and Humphrey's pretty ones that led President Hopkins to pass the baton to John Sloan Dickey with a single piece of advice: "Never have anything to do with murals."

Dartmouth people are forever setting watches. It may be the college's oldest tradition. In undergraduates it is, perhaps, a natural expression of the growing conscience. When the students burned the barn, for instance, they also rose as one to petition the hesitant trustees to admit the college's first black applicant. During the Civil War, Dartmouth undergraduates exploded over President Lord's pronouncement that slavery was "divinely ordained"—and then they helped the trustees engineer his resignation. In 1917, they demanded from a reluctant administration a military officer to teach them to march so they could—and did—go off to die with half the seed of Europe.

When the town instituted a student poll tax, the students paid up, packed the town meeting, and voted in a new town hall 500 feet tall and 6 feet square. The tax went away. One mad spring day in 1930, 2,200 Dartmouth students donned skivvies and hacked-off trousers in a "furious revolt" against long pants that made Fox-Movietone News and is still a mystery. Late in the thirties, the faculty cancelled classes when 400 men of Dartmouth held an anti-war demonstration, flirting with pacifism—and their friends from Smith, who travelled up to march as the Future Gold Star Mothers of America. ❧❧❧

You would think the fury of aerial bombardment
Would rouse God to relent; the infinite spaces
Are still silent. He looks on shock-pried faces.
History, even, does not know what is meant.

Do not expect that you will make any lasting or very strong impression on the world through intellectual power without the use of an equal amount of conscience and heart.

꙰꙰꙰ August 1945. Hiroshima. Nagasaki. The world changed utterly.

New generations of students put aside raging at the moon and consecrated themselves to saving the earth. They listened to Gandhi, sang with Martin Luther King, read Betty Friedan, grew more and more anxious about Vietnam. President Dickey, sensing the change, tried to explain it. "Do not judge the college student of today by the standards of yesterday," he warned. "Remember that he is different, faced with graver issues than we were a generation ago, more responsible in his decisions—and much more lonely."

Even Mr. Dickey was surprised, though, in May of 1969 when students, urging him to reflect on the latest war they were being asked to die in, occupied his Parkhurst office for 12 hours. Elders were outraged. "Mob violence!" they cried, and judges handed down stiff sentences, which were everywhere applauded.

Neither a mob nor violent, the students went peaceably to their cells, with but one benediction: "The behavior of the young is sometimes incomprehensible," wrote a Maine newspaper editor. "But the response of the older generation is as often inexplicable."

Cambodia—new war abroad. Watts, Detroit, Berkeley, Kent State—war at home. Some of the elders began to listen. One of them was Dartmouth's new, European-born president. He had faith in young people, and he shared their urgency. "This is a generation of students devoted, dedicated and highly impatient," John Kemeny explained to angry alumni in May of 1970. "It knows it does not have a hundred years—knows that there are clear and present dangers to the survival of civilization."

Deputized by destiny, Kemeny was leading the College forward as befits a place of learning. "Unlike other campuses, which are in flames over this issue," he told his audience, "we are going to have a highly dignified protest on Tuesday morning."

It was the first of many such protests that John Kemeny and his successors would preside over in the coming years: protests against war, and protests over the absence of women, over the presence of women, the treatment of women, the treatment of blacks, the Indian symbol, apartheid. Protests over the protests. Not all were dignified, for, as Mr. Dickey had foretold, "A college must learn as it goes and go as it learns—and a healthy college being a somewhat ornery creature, all that learning and all that going are not likely to be in one direction."

The moral and the moonstruck may at last be travelling in the same direction though—at least among students and faculty. Recently, they began again to protest college investments in South Africa. One windy fall morning a group of students struggled onto the Green lugging an African shanty. At once, the big bronze doors of Parkhurst opened, and a dean strode solemnly down the steps.

"If you put that thing on the ground," he warned, "it's a structure. There's a town ordinance against structures on the Green."

There was a moment. Then, respectfully, a student spoke.

"What if we hold it up?"

"Then it's a sign."

"Is there an ordinance against signs on the Green?"

"No."

There was another moment. Hard to tell what was going on behind the dean's moustache. But the student was grinning when he turned to his companions and hollered, "Hey, guys! Don't drop it. It's a sign!"

S.G.

The crucible in which fine words are reduced to truth, or to nothing.

Light Motifs

*Up here we have two seasons—nine months of
winter and three months of late-in-the-fall.*

Down from black emptiness they come gleaming,
thick wet swarming clumps, and vanish into black
pavement, as though we were swimming through
the Milky Way and out the far side.

Next morning: slop.

*Luminous morning. Life shimmers. A perfect gray
birch feeling the turn — the spot-rumped foal in
Vern Drew's pasture whirling its tail as it
suckles — a bright brown dog, sitting motionless, ears
forward, in a bright green meadow — cleaving cells
dropping onto the glassy river from a sculler's oars.
Over everything a pale pearl sky endless with yes.*

Playfields

*The fruits of wisdom are more obtainable for him
who saunters than for him who runs along the road
of knowledge.*

North is weather, winter, and change:
a wind-shift, snow, and how ice ages
shape the moraine of a mountain range.

At tree line the chiseled ledges
are ragged to climb; wind-twist trees
give way to the thrust of granite ridges,
peaks reach through abrasive centuries
of rain.

In the old days when Dartmouth lay snowbound all
winter, men did not exercise enough, livers became
clogged, the tap of the hammer was heard in the
dorms, and strong men said bitter things about the
administration.

You guys in the admissions office go at everything the wrong way. First thing you ask for is a photograph. What kind of a photograph? "Head and shoulders." Why, you can't even tell whether the guy is wearing skates.

March: that was the month that wasn't/didn't. ROTC wasn't in the news; it didn't snow much; the mud wasn't more than waist-deep; the robins didn't return; St. Patrick's Day wasn't unobserved; the students didn't march; the faculty wasn't obstreperous; the boilers didn't run out of oil; the College wasn't bankrupt; the Connecticut didn't flood; the Riverside Grill wasn't open; the basketball team didn't lose a game; there wasn't a daffodil in sight for Passover or Easter. It was March.

Men have invented many ways to do the devil's work, and it sometimes takes a little while for a society to see through the most recent contraptions for creating hell on earth.

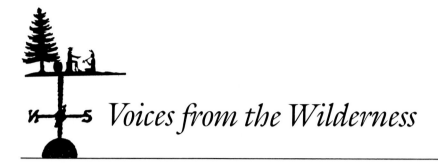

Voices from the Wilderness

1770

Sometimes he must have wondered—camped late in the year on a riverbank miles upstream from anywhere, in the crowding gloom of pine, in downed timber and choking smoke, the Reverend Wheelock must have wondered at God's ways.

Twenty-five years devoted to Christianizing the Indians had failed. His little school in Connecticut—for all his zeal, for all the support of people like Ben Franklin and the Earl of Dartmouth and the King himself—was dying. Prospects of starting anew in Pennsylvania or Massachusetts had come to nothing. He was 59.

Governor Wentworth had offered him 500 acres here in the north country. So he would start over, dare one last deed for the Redeemer, build a college from a pine forest. Bring the Indian school, of course, but build now a college for all comers. Train missionaries. In what seemed a "horrid Wilderness" he would lift up his voice again.

Whatever mixed purposes carried him north—stubborn faith, vision, self-interest, desperation—Eleazar Wheelock had only his tough old spirit to rely upon, and a few hands, red and white, to help. It had to be that way: the two peoples working together, starting something never done before.

Later, when the cabins were up, the students would live and learn together, reciting their lessons, studying, praying, eating, enduring the long snows together. Thus, from the goodness of his soul, Eleazar founded his log college, in a working brotherhood of Indians and whites.

Trust begets trust. In 1774, 21 Indians, 10 from Canada, came to enroll. But the Revolution obliterated all that. In the century following, Dartmouth graduated fewer than a dozen Native Americans. The vision faded, became a remote tradition, an incantation.

"A college founded for Indians." The saying was never wholly true, but the spell remained—its promise, like whispers of wind in the pines, troubling our spirits a-midnight.

Then suddenly Hovey—poet, vagabond, maker and shaker of histories. Richard Hovey, Class of 1885, wished only to salute the Reverend Founder in a rollicking camp-fire song. Instead he breathed life into the ancient words, and created a legendary chief *answering* from the wilderness. Here, yes, was a proud young red man, quite the equal of the venerable white tutor. The red chief and the white chief sat them down. Loudly the two harangued, grandly they gesticulated—and founded Dartmouth College.

It must be true. It's all written down.

Hovey's Sachem was a magical symbol. The undergraduates whooped at the song's irreverence; and the alumni, remembering their years of zest, felt the old bones stir. Eventually—in the shorthand of sports writers—the athletic teams became "Indians," and vendors of all sorts began to turn mythology into money.

But history's an insomniac. Was there nothing to the Dartmouth Indian beyond a saying and a song? When that question was asked, Americans—red, white, black, brown, yellow—were stumbling together through the jungles of Southeast Asia. There we caught the afterglow of our own worst history: long houses and lodges in flames across the centuries. From the burning of the Pequots in 1630 to the last betrayed stragglers at Wounded Knee—250 years of it, till all the land was fenced, till all the tribes were dispersed, broken, civilized.

1970

Dartmouth, now a large college, or a small university, inaugurated a new president. Out of the drab tyrannies of Eastern Europe came an old-world scholar, courtly, humane, a brilliant mathematician and teacher. John Kemeny knew what it was to be silenced in an occupied homeland. At Dartmouth he proposed three liberating changes: let blacks be further encouraged to enroll; open the college to women; and awaken Eleazar's original vision. "I hereby pledge my energies to the effort of translating the long-deferred promise of Dartmouth's Charter into reality." The trustees backed him.

None of these changes was easy, but it was especially difficult to persuade young Indians to return. Few were schooled for the work and not one wanted to symbolize anything. The first Americans, men and women they were—not mascots.

Nonetheless some came, trusting once again. Silently they came, warily, to this unfamiliar territory, bewildered like any freshmen and feeling a terrible long way from home. Fortunately, at this moment, a Modoc-American anthropologist was appointed to design a Native American Studies program. The program has grown into a national model, illuminating the suppressed but inseparable histories of Euro-Americans and Native Americans.

Ancient elemental American names: Tuscarora, Comanche, Seneca, Cherokee, Chippewa, Micmac, Arikara, Shoshone—names that once sent whites scrambling for flintlocks. Since 1970, one hundred and three tribes have sent young men and women to Dartmouth.

Sleep well, Eleazar.

Hovey, rejoice us a new song.

D.B., S.G.

Abenaki • Aleut • Algonquin • Apache • Arapaho • Arikara • Assiniboin • Athabascan • Bannock • Blackfeet • Caddo • Cayuga • Chemehuevi • Cherokee • Cheyenne • Chickasaw • Chippewa • Choctaw • Cochiti • Coeur d'Alene • Colville • Comanche • Coos • Cree • Creek • Croate • Crow • Delaware • Eskimo • Flathead • Fox • Hawaiian • Hidatsa • Hoopa • Hopi • Houma • Inupiaq • Iowa • Isleta • Karok • Kiowa • Laguna • Lakota • Lumbee • Makah • Mandan • Mayan • Menominee • Mesquakie • Miami • Micmac • Miwok • Modoc • Mohawk • Nanticoke • Narragansett • Navajo • Nez Perce • Nipmuc • Ojibway • Omaha • Oneida • Onondaga • Osage • Otoe • Ottowa • Paiute • Passamaquoddy • Pawnee • Penobscot • Peoria • Pima • Pomo • Potawatomi • Quilute • Rappahannock • Sac & Fox • Salish • San Juan • Santa Clara • Schaghticoke • Seminole • Seneca • Shinnecock • Shoshone • Siletz • Sioux • Skokomish • Spokane • Taos • Tlingit • Tohono O'otham • Tuscarora • Ute • Wailaki • Wampanoag • Winnebago • Yakima • Yaqui • Yuki • Yupik • Yurok • Zuni

Celebrations

They who miss the joy miss all.

Dartmouth has never been effete. As early as 1828, thirty-one students were fined two dollars each for attending a dancing school.

Hello—
I really hate this place. There's really nothing to report. Carnival will be terrible, the weather is terrible, the books are terrible, the food is terrible, I'm not sleeping well, and the whole world seems totally worthless.

Goodbye.

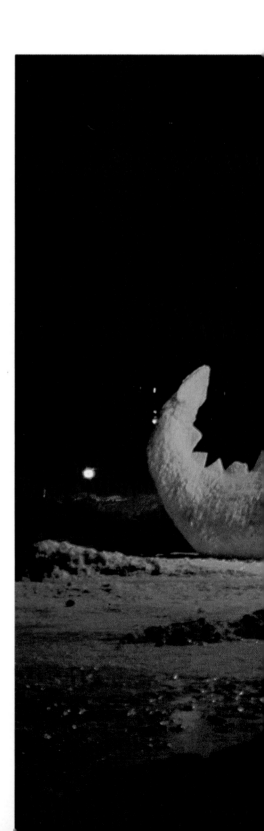

A place most favorable and friendly to the studies of youth . . . free from a thousand snares, temptations, and divertissements.

Accident

*After six months in Washington, you can't imagine
how nice it is to return to civilization.*

Sometimes it all makes sense. . . . I think of those rare periods of life when everything clicked together, where larger patterns could be seen, and when I felt fully awake to being alive. I remember walking at four in the morning to put up kilometer markings for Carnival and stopping to gaze into the clear sky and feeling the magnificence of the stars. I think of a conversation at the Outward Bound shelter, about the threat of nuclear annihilation, while the tranquility of a nearby lake served as an anchor against despair. . . . Or anytime when the world looked cleaner, and life tingled and became less of a chore.

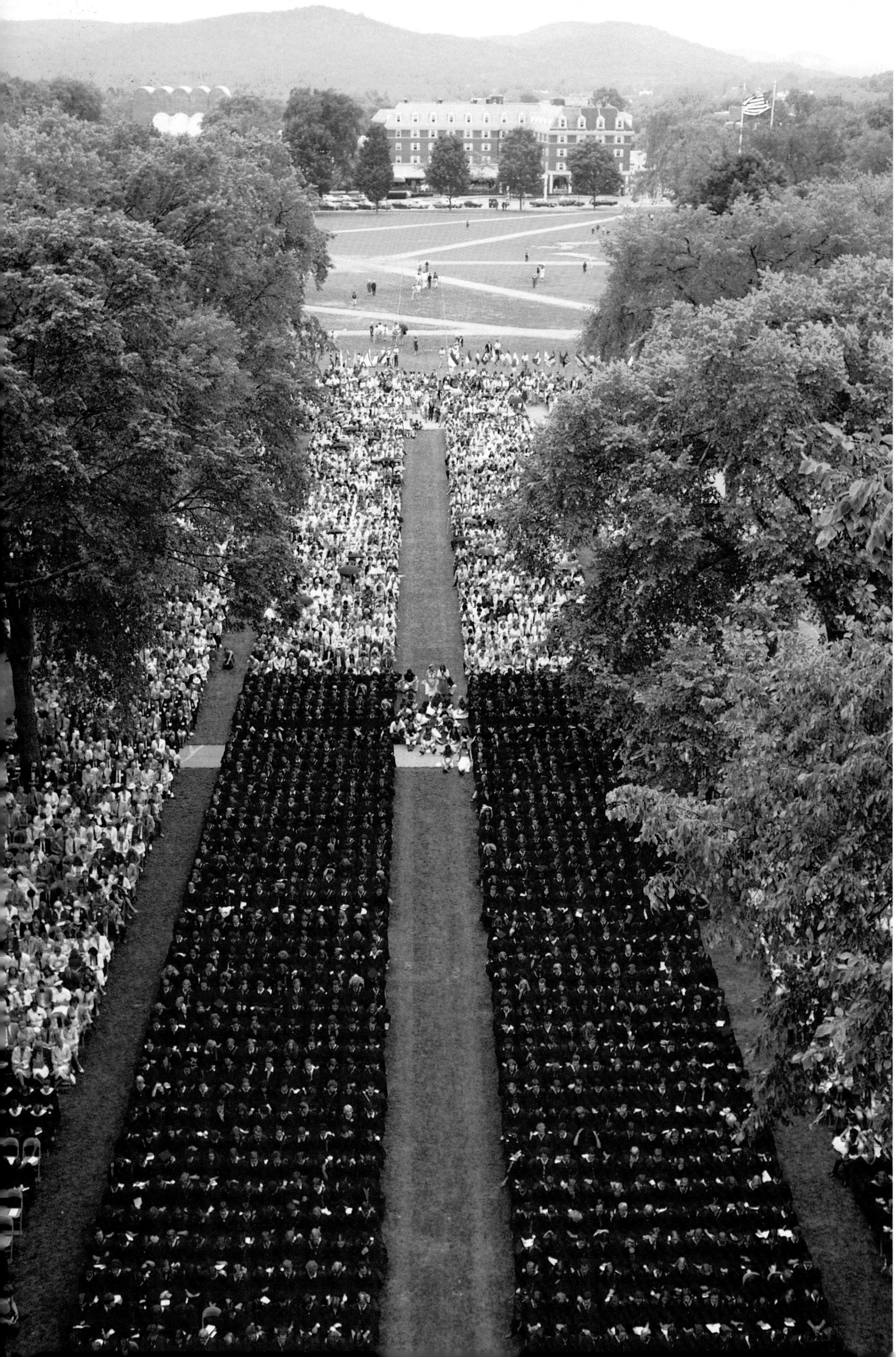

From Here On

I'm not a religious man . . . but I think every man has to give worship to something bigger than himself, and Dartmouth College is a good enough religion for me.

From here on — to the end of the road — the choice of the good, the beautiful, the true will be made for you only if made by you.

Thomas W. Ames, Jr. (Lebanon, New Hampshire) is an advertising photographer with a studio in Lebanon, and a wife and two children in Thetford Center, Vermont.

Anne M. Arquit '84, a campus photographer, was editor-in-chief of the 1984 *Aegis*. After graduation, she took a doctorate at the University of Hawaii.

Philip Booth '47 (Castine, Maine) Eight books of poetry, including *Relations and Selected Poems 1950–1985;* his first book won the Lamont Prize of the Academy of American Poets, which elected him a Fellow in 1985. Awards from *Poetry* and The National Institute of Arts and Letters, and Rockefeller and Guggenheim Fellowships.

Adrian N. Bouchard (1911–1983) Ski jumper, ski teacher, bellhop, photographer from Berlin, New Hampshire. Three and a half years in the Pacific war, then back as Dartmouth's official college photographer. Most ubiquitous and joyful of Dartmouth men, and an honorary member of the Class of 1941.

Stuart Bratesman '75 (White River Junction, Vermont) Born in Manhattan, raised in Hanover, and graduated from Dartmouth with a major in history. His pictures have appeared in *Time, Newsweek, U.S. News, Sports Illustrated, Rolling Stone,* and in books by Hunter Thompson, Frances Fitzgerald, Gary Hart, and Georges Seldes. College photographer at Dartmouth since 1985.

William Bronk '38 (Hudson Falls, New York) Poet-essayist. Born 1918.

Gary Davis (Wakefield, Massachusetts) Artist and illustrator, he made his reputation as an ad designer for CBS, Rebok, IBM, Harvard.

Richard Eberhart '26 (Hanover, New Hampshire) Tutor in the household of the King of Siam, long-time poet-in-residence at Dartmouth. Pultizer, Bollingen, and National Book awards, member of the American Academy of Arts and Letters and the American Academy of Arts and Sciences. Recently: *Collected Poems 1930–1986* and *Marine Poems,* both Oxford University Press.

Corey Ford (1902-1969) Colonel in the U.S.A.F., owned by English setter "Cider." Son of Columbia U., adopted son of Dartmouth. Prolific essayist, humorist, satirist, parodist. He founded and for 15 years financed the Rugby Club at Dartmouth.

Jon Gilbert Fox (Norwich, Vermont) Name a gallery or exhibition in Vermont or New Hampshire, a newspaper or magazine in New York or Washington, a festival or arts project from the Washington Ballet to the San Diego Opera, and he'll be there. Now freelance and with the *Dartmouth Alumni Magazine.*

Robert Frost Class of 1896 (1874–1963) Poet, teacher, lecturer. He spent two and a half months as a freshman at Dartmouth. Thereafter: 11 books of poetry. Forever of Amherst College, University of Michigan, Harvard, Dartmouth, and Ripton, Vermont.

Kari Heistad (Lebanon, New Hampshire) Outdoors photographer, known for her presentation of New England and European scenes. Her work has appeared in many publications, exhibitions, and craft fairs.

Dewitt Jones '65 (Bolinas, California) Well-known photographer and filmmaker whose previous books include *John Muir's America* and *Robert Frost: A Tribute to the Source.* His work appears regularly in *National Geographic* magazine, and his film *John Muir's High Sierra* was nominated for two Academy Awards.

B. A. King (Southboro, Massachusetts) A photographer of "ordinary objects and everyday events." His prints are collected in the Fogg Museum and other famous museums in this country, in Canada, and in France. Eight books, running from *Ojibwa Summer,* 1972, to *The Very Best Christmas Tree,* 1984.

Heinz Kluetmeier '65 (Milwaukee, Wisconsin) Already famed as an undergraduate photographer, now on the staff of *Sports Illustrated.* His work has appeared also in *Life, Fortune, People* and on over 100 *Sports Illustrated* covers.

Larry McDonald (Enfield, New Hampshire) Thirty-two years as professional photographer and teacher, beginning with U.S.A.F. and *Stars and Stripes* in Japan. Six professional awards and two civic awards while with the *Valley News.* Now co-owner McDonald/Dall Photography in West Lebanon, New Hampshire.

Robert Meservey '43 (Lexington, Massachusetts) Dartmouth ski captain and architectural photographer. Now research physicist at M.I.T. specializing in superconductivity.

John Moragné '79 (San Francisco, California) Degrees from Dartmouth and Stanford; consultant with Bain & Co., San Francisco; expert kayaker and canoeist.

Tim Morse (Carlisle, Massachusetts) Freelance photographer exhibited at the Smithsonian and published in *Sports Illustrated* and *Newsweek*. Sports photographer for Harvard College and other Boston schools, U.S. Olympic Committee, and NCAA. Staff photographer for *Swimming World*.

Jeffrey Nintzel '73 (Plainfield, New Hampshire) Known especially for high-class photographs of pictures, statues, art objects. On call at the Hood Museum of Art.

Art Phaneuf (Plainfield, New Hampshire) Stock photographer and photojournalist for national magazines and textbooks, who specializes in people, their traditions and lifestyles, as well as celebrities, political and sport figures. Represented by Animals Animals/Earth Scenes in New York City.

Robert Rattner (Richmond Hill, New York) Travel, nature, and underwater photographer whose work has appeared in many national magazines, among them *The New Yorker, Smithsonian, National Geographic*. Now working on a book about manatees.

George A. Robinson (South Burlington, Vermont) Trained at Brooks Institute in Santa Barbara, he became an industrial photographer for General Electric in Burlington; he freelanced for such books as *Dartmouth—A Visual Remembrance, Cornell*, and *Beautiful Vermont*.

Marilyn S. Rogers (Lebanon, New Hampshire) Once a secretary at *The Daily Dartmouth*, she is now a freelance photographer publishing in *Vermont Life*.

Len Rubenstein (Easton, Massachusetts) Born of Hungary and Brooklyn, Len found photography during an M.F.A. at the University of Connecticut. He has taken pictures for MIT, Fortune 500, the YWCA—but it was photographing autistic children at the Higashi School that made an artist of him.

Paul Sample '21 (1896–1974) Heavyweight boxing champ and swing saxophonist at Dartmouth. Tuberculosis brought him to painting, talent brought him fame, Mr. Hopkins brought him home: to 24 years as artist-in-residence.

Carol Selikowitz (Etna, New Hampshire) Formerly a teacher of photography at Lewis and Clark College, she is now a contributing editor for *New Hampshire Profiles*. Her photographs illustrate Van Schaik's book on dressage.

Kathryn Sheehan (Grantham, New Hampshire) A photographer since eight, she works in nature, wildlife, and industrial photography and has won numerous awards for her unusual and delicate work.

John S. Sheldon '74 (Norwich, Vermont) Well-known local photographer for many years, he now operates a commercial studio, *Hathorn/Olson Photographers*, in Hartford, Vermont.

William M. Smith (Hanover, New Hampshire) Professor of Psychology, Director of Instructional Services at Dartmouth, author of many scientific papers, co-author of the books *The Behavior of Man* and *Perception and Motion*, producer of three video discs on perception.

Ralph Steiner '21 (1899–1986) Pioneering American artist in black-and-white stills and motion pictures—one of the first to bring photography to fruition as sharp and speaking art. Born in Ohio, Steiner was a master of technique and an indomitably joyous spirit. He worked in New York and Hollywood, then in Maine and Vermont, where he died just before the opening of a last exhibition entitled "In Spite of Everything, Yes."

Mark Stern (Orford, New Hampshire) From biology he turned to photography, studying under John Shaw, Sam Abell, and Dorothea Keyaya. Wide recognition in many contests and exhibits in northern New England.

Marc Teatum (Salem, Massachusetts) of Brooklyn, Parsons School of Design, Morgan Library, Dartmouth. Now owns a studio and commercial ad business. Pictures in *Smithsonian, Harvard*, and *National Geographic* magazines.

Nancy Wasserman '77 (Montpelier, Vermont) Last of Bouchard's student assistants, she learned to catch the flow of action and developed an instinct to be there when things happen. Photographer of the college for years, editor, and publisher, she now manages the Vermont Community Loan Fund.

Identifications and Credits

25 The campus, 1883, William M. Notman/Dartmouth College Library.

Dartmouth Hall burns for the second time, 1904, Dartmouth College Library.

26 Bartlett quotation from *The College on the Hill*, p. 80. Patten quotation from Edward Connery Lathem's *The Dartmouth Experience*, pp. 50–51.

Professor of Biology William Patten, who designed the "Evolution" survey course for freshmen in the twenties and thirties, 1922, Dartmouth College Library.

27 President Ernest Martin Hopkins '01, c. 1930, A. Burton Street.

Presidential limousine, c. 1940, Dartmouth College Photographic Records.

Hoppy loved everything about being president—from greeting the freshmen to speaking to alumni—and he wanted for Dartmouth the best teachers he could entice to Hanover.

28 Fan vaulting, 1946, Adrian Bouchard.

29 Lines from "Midsummer" by William Bronk '38, in *The World, The Worldless*, New Directions, San Francisco Review Press, 1964.

30 President Hopkins quotation from *Hopkins of Dartmouth* by Charles Widmayer '30, 1977, p. 151.

Classroom on the Row, then and now, taken in 1972 by Stuart Bratesman '75.

David Lambuth, Professor of English, c. 1945, Dartmouth College Library. The words are his.

31 Conversation adapted from *Hopkins of Dartmouth*, p. 113.

Baker a-building, 1927, Dartmouth College Library.

32–33 Winter campus, c. 1948, Adrian Bouchard.

Baker Library cost, in the end, $1,132,000; Mr. Baker, pleased with Jens Fredrick Larson's design, set aside another million for furnishings and maintenance. The family of Professor of English Edwin David Sanborn, Class of 1832, contributed Sanborn House and yet another $1,300,000 for books.

Story adapted from *Hopkins of Dartmouth*, p. 113.

34 Climber, 1947, Robert Meservey '43. The Dartmouth Mountaineering Club was created in 1938 and sometimes stretched a rope on Vermont's Fairlee cliffs.

Memorial Field, 1925, Ralph Steiner '21. This team (which included four members of Phi Beta Kappa) defeated Chicago to become national champions.

35 Corey Ford's description of a Bataan Christmas, 1942, from *The College on the Hill*, p. 256.

Navy V-12s passing in review, 1943, Dartmouth College Library.

36 Reserve Reading Room of Baker, 1979, Dartmouth College Photographic Records. Here, in 3,000 magnificent square feet, is the famous mural study of Mexican and American history painted by José Clemente Orozco. The work, completed in 1934, took two years.

Story adapted from Edward Connery Lathem's *Ernest Martin Hopkins on His Dartmouth Presidential Years*, 1987.

37 *Gods of the Modern World* from *The Epic of American Civilization*, fresco by José Clemente Orozco, Mexican, 1932–34. Courtesy of the Trustees of Dartmouth College.

38 Dartmouth Hall at dusk, 1984, Marilyn S. Rogers.

President Hopkins' wish, after a visit to Oxford and Cambridge, recounted in *Hopkins of Dartmouth*, p. 114.

39 President John Sloan Dickey '29 on the job, 1951, Adrian Bouchard.

President Dickey understood that at their best, teaching and research were inseparable and self-replenishing. His seminal innovation was the Great Issues course, for which he sought experts, national and international, in all fields. The idea lives on in the Montgomery Fellowships and the Dickey Endowment for International Understanding.

Jason, who owned Bouch, 1974, Adrian Bouchard.

Corey Ford's story from "My Dog Likes It Here," excerpted in *Dartmouth Alumni Magazine,* May 1978.

40 The work that never stays done, 1978, Nancy Wasserman '77.

President Dickey dedicating the new artificial ice in Davis Rink, 1953, Adrian Bouchard.

Walter Prager, coach from 1937 to 1957, taken in 1948 by Robert Meservey '43.

President Dwight D. Eisenhower, speaking at Dartmouth Commencement 1953.

41 Rollins and Baker towers, 1986, Nancy Wasserman '77.

42 Robert Frost writing in the introduction to *Dartmouth Verse,* 1925.

Students, 1966, Dartmouth College Photographic Records.

43 Robert Frost, c. 1962, Heinz Kluetmeier '65.

44 Leonard M. Rieser '44, 1987, Bratesman/Dartmouth College.

The versatile physicist, whiz kid at Los Alamos, has labored for four Dartmouth presidents — as professor, as dean of the faculty, as provost, now Fairchild Professor of Natural Sciences and Director of the Dickey Endowment for International Understanding.

Thaddeus Seymour, Dean of the College from 1959 to 1969, taken in 1967 by Adrian Bouchard.

Hopkins Center for the Performing Arts, 1988, © Robert Rattner.

President Dickey's second act in office, in 1945, was to plan an arts center. The Hop opened its doors in 1962, 17 years later — 40 years after Drama Coach Warner Bentley had been promised "a theater."

45 Mr. Dickey with roses, 1969, Adrian Bouchard.

President Dickey speaking at Commencement 1947.

46 President John G. Kemeny, Commencement 1981, Marc Teatum.

47 Lines from "North," by Philip Booth '47, in *Selected Poems 1950–1985,* Viking Press, 1986.

Neither snow nor rain nor heat nor gloom of grades . . . , 1986, Bratesman/Dartmouth College.

48 Man at work, 1985, Bratesman/Dartmouth College.

Woman at work, 1989, Jon Gilbert Fox.

49 Brave new world, 1987, Thomas W. Ames Jr./Thayer School.

Lines from "Twilight Song" by Fred Lewis Pattee, Class of 1888, in *Dartmouth Songbook,* 1950, p. 70.

50 Tropical ecology in Costa Rica, 1982, Anne M. Arquit '84.

Class in the Colliseum, Rome, c. 1983, Dartmouth College Photographic Records.

51 Architect's rendering of Dartmouth-Hitchcock Medical Center, Lebanon Road, 1989.

Kresge Fitness Room, Berry Sports Center, 1989, Jon Gilbert Fox.

52   Lake Dartmouth, 1988, Jon Gilbert Fox.

Morton, Zimmerman, and Andres dormitories—opened in 1986—make up the East Wheelock Cluster, 1988, Nancy Wasserman '77.

53   The portals of Memorial Field—through which pass the most devoted alumni in the world, 1980, Nancy Wasserman '77.

Hanover, New Hampshire, date unknown, Dartmouth College Photographic Records.

54   Professors: Walter Stockmayer of Chemistry, 1978, Nancy Wasserman '77. Blanche Gelfant of English, c. 1980, Dartmouth College Photographic Records. James Cox of English, 1978, Adrian Bouchard.

55   Professors: Charles T. Wood of History, 1978, Adrian Bouchard. Priscilla Sears of English, 1985, B. A. King. John Rassias of French and Italian, 1985, B. A. King. Vincent Starzinger of Government, 1975, Adrian Bouchard.

56   Professor of History Marysa Navarro and student, 1979, Stuart Bratesman.

President Dickey speaking at Commencement 1956.

Woeful student, 1977, Adrian Bouchard.

57   Design class, 1966, Adrian Bouchard.

58–59   Professor of Geography Robert E. Huke '48 in class, Mt. Washington, 1972, Adrian Bouchard.

60   Professor of Environmental Economics L. Greg Hines and senior entering Escape Rapids, Coppermine River, above the Arctic Circle, 1979, John Moragné '79.

61   President Dickey, speaking at Convocation 1954.

Hood Museum of Art, 1986, courtesy of the museum.

Assyrian reliefs and Greek amphora from the permanent collection at the Hood Museum of Art, 1987, © Robert Rattner.

62   Three presidents—McLaughlin, Kemeny, Dickey—1981, Nancy Wasserman '77.

President Dickey to President-elect Kemeny, 1970.

Jean Kemeny, Chris Dickey, Judy McLaughlin at the McLaughlin inauguration, 1981, John Sheldon/Hathorn-Olson.

63   From President Freedman's inaugural address, 1987.

President James O. Freedman, 1988, Bratesman/Dartmouth College.

64   Medical students, 1988, Stuart Bratesman '75.

Nathan Smith, a Harvard Medical School graduate, founded Dartmouth's medical school, the fourth in the country, in 1797. For many years he was the whole curriculum.

65   The door of the Thayer School of Engineering, just before expansion got it, 1988, Wasserman/Thayer School. The school was founded in 1871 by General Sylvanus Thayer, Class of 1807, designer and superintendent of the modern West Point.

Engineering students at work on a prize-winning solar-powered car, 1988, Wasserman/Thayer School.

66   James Brian Quinn, Professor of Management and everything else, Amos Tuck School, 1985, Stuart Bratesman '75.

The Amos Tuck School of Business Administration, 1984, John Sheldon/Hathorn-Olson. Edward Tuck, Class of 1861, was William Jewett Tucker's roommate in College and later Dartmouth's great benefactor. In 1900 he created the first graduate school of business in the country—Tuck—to honor his father, Class of 1835.

67   Reminiscence of Erich Segal, in "Myths About Dartmouth," *Dartmouth Alumni Magazine,* September 1976.

February midnight, 1982, Professor William M. Smith.

69 *Daniel Webster (Black Dan)*, oil on canvas by Francis Alexander, American, 1835. Gift of Dr. G. C. Shattuck, Class of 1803, to the College — now in permanent collection at the Hood Museum.

Shorts Rebellion, 1930, Dartmouth College Library.

70 Lines from "The Fury of Aerial Bombardment," by Richard Eberhart '26, *Collected Poems* 1930, 1986. Reprinted by permission of Oxford University Press and the author.

Arrests, Parkhurst occupation over ROTC and Vietnam War, May 1969, Larry McDonald/*Valley News.*

71 Arrests, shantytown demonstration against apartheid, February 1986, Dartmouth College Photographic Records.

Shantytown, raised by students protesting Dartmouth investments in South Africa and razed by students protesting the protest, fall 1985, Bratesman/Dartmouth College.

President Tucker quoted by President Dickey in "Conscience and the Undergraduate," *Atlantic Monthly,* April 1955.

73 Russell Sage Hall, 1974, Adrian Bouchard.

74–75 David T. McLaughlin '54, President of the College 1981–87, and students during the second occupation of Parkhurst, over both racism on campus and apartheid, January 1986, all Bratesman/Dartmouth College.

76 Fall, 1988, Kathryn Sheehan.

77 Winter signature, 1988, © Mark Stern.

Words by Robert Frost, Class of 1896.

78 Slop, 1979, Professor William M. Smith.

79 Spring, 1986, Kathryn Sheehan.

80 Summer pond, 1988, © Mark Stern.

81 Lucky eight, 1974, Adrian Bouchard.

82 Hikers on Moosilauke, 1981, Nancy Wasserman '77.

President Hopkins quotation from *Hopkins of Dartmouth,* p. 163.

83 Harvard team, circa forever, Dartmouth College Photographic Records.

Sometimes it is hard, 1984, Nancy Wasserman '77.

Hip and helmet, 1984, John Sheldon/Hathorn-Olson.

84–85 Mt. Washington, first shiver, 1988, Kari Heistad.

Lines from "North" by Philip Booth '47, in *Relations,* copyright © 1986 by Philip Booth. All rights reserved. Reprinted by permission of Viking Penguin, a division of Penguin Books USA, Inc.

86–87 Occom Pond, c. 1961, Adrian Brueghel.

Editorial words from Boston *Evening Transcript,* 1930.

Immortal plaint of hockey coach Eddie Jeremiah, from *Selected Writings* by Dean of Freshmen Albert Inskip Dickerson, 1974, p. 207.

Hockey, situation normal, 1977, John Sheldon/Hathorn-Olson.

88 Downhill skier, c. 1960, Dartmouth College Photographic Records.

Skiway workers, 1956, Adrian Bouchard.

89 Cross-country on the golf course, 1983, George A. Robinson.

90 Kayak slalom, 1987, Marilyn S. Rogers.

91   Mud-season report by Dennis A. Dinan '61, editor, *Dartmouth Alumni Magazine,* April 1975.

Ivy League champion, 1984, Tim Morse.

92   Lacrosse, Chase Field, 1988, Jon Gilbert Fox.

President Dickey, speaking at Convocation 1954.

Compleat angler, 1983, George A. Robinson.

93   Carle Geer '80 (stern) and Judy Geer '75 (bow), national champions, Olympic medalists, 1982, Nancy Wasserman '77.

94   "Appeal to the Great Spirit" by Cyrus E. Dallin, 1989, Jeffrey Nintzel. This miniature of the life-sized 1912 bronze at the Museum of Fine Arts in Boston was given to the College in 1928 by Leslie P. Snow, Class of 1886. It still watches over the Tower Room of Baker Library.

96   The Dartmouth College Glee Club, Paul Zeller directing, 1965, Adrian Bouchard.

97   President Hopkins quoting Robert Louis Stevenson in 1945, *Hopkins of Dartmouth,* p. 294.

Adrian Bouchard, College photographer, 1977, Dartmouth College Photographic Records.

98   Building the bonfire, 1988, © Art Phaneuf/Camera Shop of Hanover.

Red Smith quotation from *Saturday Evening Post,* 1949.

Embers, 1968, Adrian Bouchard.

99   Christmas, 1972, Adrian Bouchard.

Mellerdramer at the Hop, circa anytime, Dartmouth Alumni College Archives.

100   Flakey engineers, Winter Carnival 1987, Bratesman/Dartmouth College.

Freshman letter home, quoted by Dean Dickerson in his *Selected Writings,* 1974, p. 179.

101   Winter Carnival statue, 1969, Adrian Bouchard.

102   Citizens' Classic ski race, Carnival 1987, Bratesman/Dartmouth College.

103   Eleazar Wheelock quotation from *The College on the Hill,* p. 80.

Accident at Carnival, 1988, Bratesman/Dartmouth College.

104   Pepe de Chiazza and Jerry Zaks '67 in *L'histoire du Soldat,* Hopkins Center, 1976, Stuart Bratesman '75.

Dancers, Powwow 1988, © Art Phaneuf/Camera Shop of Hanover.

105   Charioteers, 1983, George A. Robinson.

President Kemeny's opening statement upon his return from chairing the Three Mile Island Commission, *Dartmouth Alumni Magazine,* December 1980.

Muzuk, 1986, Bratesman/Dartmouth College.

At first they were literary societies — and, thanks to departing seniors, often the best, most disorganized libraries in the college. By 1850 they were converting to fraternities with Greek names and spooky rituals. Joined now by sororities, they still seek an acceptable Attic mix of literature, libation, and libido in their best-of-all-college worlds.

106   The Dartmouth Symphony Orchestra in Spaulding Auditorium, Hopkins Center, 1978, Stuart Bratesman '75.

107   Sean Murphy '88, musing in the Dartmouth Outing Club's "Woodsmoke," 1988.

Fred Harris and friends started the DOC in 1911. There had always been nonhibernators, from John Ledyard on, and many midwinter festivals. But Harris hit on the right words — "Winter Carnival."